A Family in Nigeria

LIBRARY OF CONGRESS CATALOGING IN PUBLICATION DATA

Barker, Carol.
 A family in Nigeria.

 Rev. ed. of: Village in Nigeria. 1984.
 Summary: Describes the life of Thaddeus, a twelve-
year-old boy who lives in a Nigerian village.
 1. Nigeria—Social life and customs—Juvenile
literature. 2. Children—Nigeria—Juvenile literature.
[1. Nigeria—Social life and customs] I. Barker, Carol.
Village in Nigeria.   II. Title.
DT515.4.B37 1985   966.9   85-6932
ISBN 0-8225-1659-4 (lib. bdg.)

Manufactured in the United States of America

1 2 3 4 5 6 7 8 9 10 95 94 93 92 91 90 89 88 87 86 85

A Family in Nigeria

Carol Barker

Lerner Publications Company • Minneapolis

Thaddeus is 12. He lives with his parents and the rest of his family in a small village in southern Nigeria. Aye-Ekan, his village, is in the state of Kwara.

Thaddeus's father is Chief Afolayan. He is one of several chiefs who help run the village. Like most people in Aye-Ekan, he is a farmer.

Thaddeus's family lives in two houses on one side of a compound. A compound is a big yard with houses grouped around it. On the other side are the houses that his uncle and uncle's family live in. The compound is called "ode-ede," which means "the most suitable place."

Thaddeus and his family are Yoruba people, one of four main groups of people in Nigeria. The other three groups are the Hausa, the Fulani, and the Ibo people.

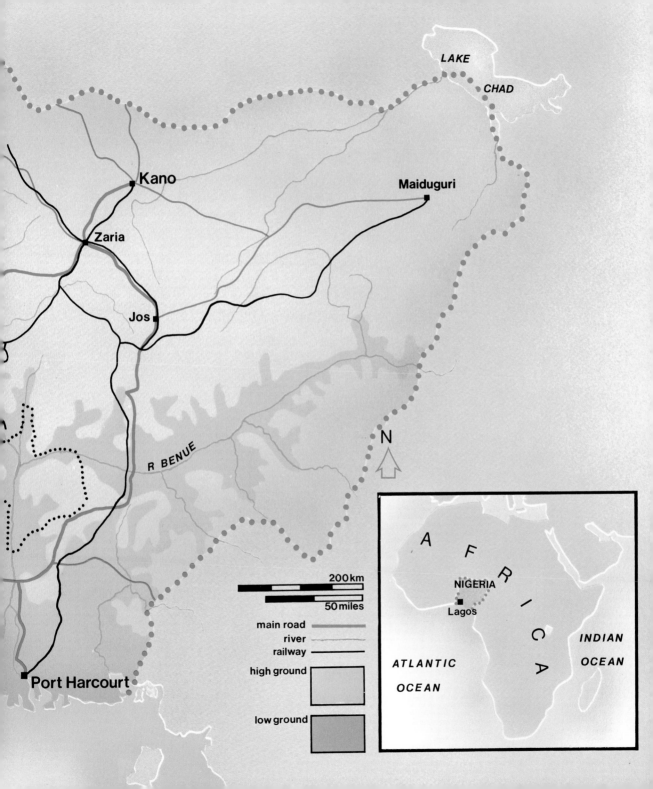

LAKE
CHAD

Kano

Maiduguri

Zaria

Jos

R BENUE

N

Port Harcourt

200 km

50 miles

main road
river
railway
high ground

low ground

AFRICA

NIGERIA

Lagos

ATLANTIC

OCEAN

INDIAN
OCEAN

Thaddeus's mother is called Aransi. Here are Thaddeus, his mother, and his father with their family and some other friends. Thaddeus's family is large because his father has six wives. Most of the men in the village have only two wives. But Chief Afolayan has three senior wives and three junior wives. Aransi is his third wife. There are sixteen children in the family but some of them have grown up and now live in other places.

Maria is the fourth wife. Aransi and the other senior wives teach the younger wives how to look after the children.

All of the women in the family work hard every day. There is no water at the compound, so the women have to walk to a river over a mile (2 kilometers) away and carry the water back in buckets. They also collect wood from the forest and chop it up to make fires for cooking.

The older children help the women prepare and cook the food. Peter, Thaddeus's brother, peels and washes the yams. When they are peeled, they will be boiled and pounded into mash. Yams are an important part of the Yoruba diet and are eaten almost every day—for breakfast, lunch, or supper. At one meal, yams might be served with a hot vegetable soup made of okra, chili peppers, and red palm nut oil. At another meal, they will be eaten with corn, beans, or green vegetables.

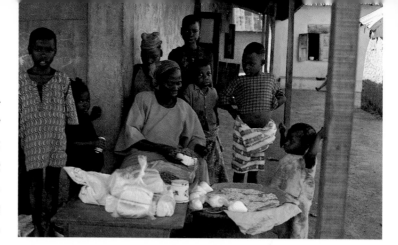

Elizabeth is Chief Afolayan's first wife. After the chief, she is the most important person in the family. On some days, she sits outside the house and sells bread, red peppers, and flour made from the cassava plants that grow on the farm.

Elizabeth and the other wives try to earn extra money besides the money earned from selling the farm produce.

Every four days, there is a market at Aye-Ekan. Aransi and the other two senior wives like to go. When they can, they will take cassava flour or ground nuts to sell. During the school holidays, Thaddeus goes with them and helps to carry the baskets.

Markets are very important in Nigeria. They are all organized and run by women. There's always so much to see at the market in Aye-Ekan. Some of the women sell live birds in baskets, while others sell palm wine, meat, fish, or cloth. There are many kinds of vegetables for sale, including corn and yams, as well as nuts, sugar cane, and bananas. You can even buy live snails and turtles!

Sometimes Aransi takes one of the junior wives to visit the Health Center in Aye-Ekan. It's open every Thursday. Women bring their babies for health and weight checks and vaccinations.

When Thaddeus was three months old, Aransi took him to the Health Center. He was vaccinated against polio, measles, whooping cough, diphtheria, and tuberculosis.

The Health Center was built in 1963 with funds raised by the people in the village. Someone is always there to give out medicines, and nurses come to visit on different days of each week. People who are very sick go to the hospital at Omu-Aran, a town about 7 miles (11 kilometers) away.

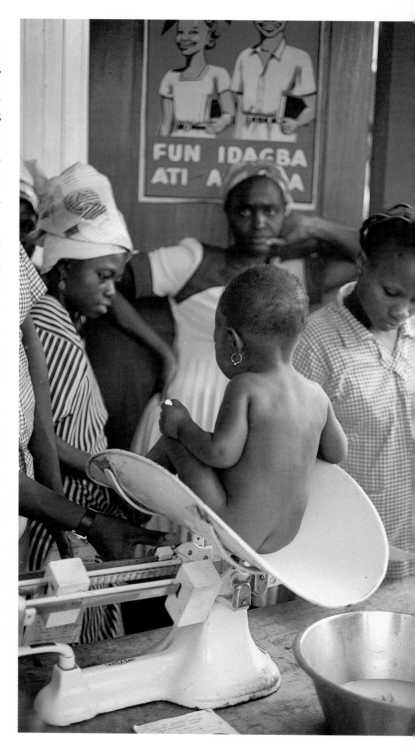

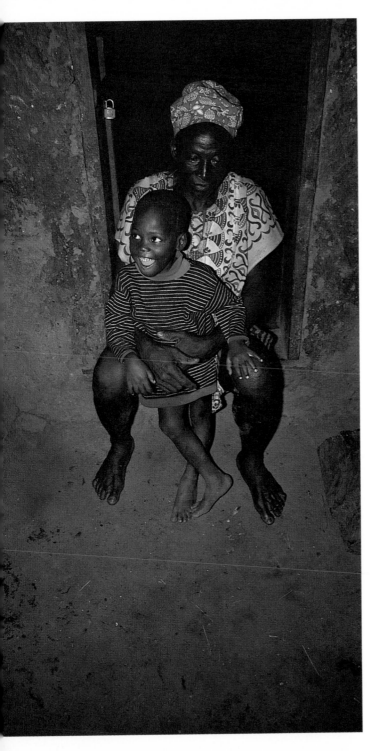

Chief Afolayan is a traditional Yoruba doctor and herbalist. He treats sick people with traditional medicines and herbs.

At first, he did not believe in modern medicines. He would not allow his senior wives to take their children to the Health Center. Aransi didn't take her first son there. But some of Thaddeus's brothers and sisters died of diseases like polio. Chief Afolayan realized that his medicines could not cure those diseases, so he let Aransi take Thaddeus to the Health Center.

People still come to Chief Afolayan for treatment and he still uses herbal medicine. He says that traditional and modern medicines should work together to cure the sick.

On Sundays, Thaddeus goes to St. Michael's Catholic Church in Aye-Ekan with some of his brothers and sisters. His uncle, Anthony Fas, is assistant to the Roman Catholic priest. When the Reverend Father is away on leave in Europe, Anthony Fas takes the church service on Sunday mornings.

When Thaddeus was a baby, he was baptized at St. Michael's. Thaddeus is being brought up as a Catholic and so are all his younger brothers and sisters. The junior wives are also Catholic. His father and mother, the other senior wives, and the older children all still follow the Yoruba gods.

This means that half the family follows the Yoruba religion and half are Christian. They are all happy living together and don't quarrel about religion. Most other families in Aye-Ekan are like Thaddeus's.

There are some Muslim people in Aye-Ekan, too. They worship in the mosque in Aye-Ekan. But there are many more Muslims in northern Nigeria than there are where Thaddeus lives.

In the old days, Yoruba people worshipped 420 gods and goddesses. But now, only the main ones are worshipped.

First in the Yoruba religion comes Olodumare, the Creator. All the other gods and goddesses are under him.

They are called Orishas (lesser gods). All the gods, except for Olodumare, have their own priests and their own festivals. The most important is Ifa, the God of Divination. His priests are diviners, called Babalawo. They tell people's fortunes.

This man is wearing an Epa mask. He's with the chief Epa priest. The Epa festival is held to worship the God of Wood and also for the spirits of the Yoruba ancestors. People believe that these spirits enter into the masks as the men are dancing.

One of the biggest festivals is for Oshun, the Goddess of the River. It's held every year at Oshogbo, near the town where the river Oshun flows. Thousands of people come to the sacred grove to worship the Goddess Oshun. There are drummers and trumpeters and a lot of dancing. Oshun is also the Goddess of Fertility. Women pray to her for children. People also pray for prosperity and collect sacred water from the river Oshun.

Aransi is a priestess of Obatala, the god who carves and molds human beings before they are born. Aransi is a leader in the festival for Obatala. Chief Afolayan follows Osanyin, the God of Medicine.

This is George Bamedele Arowogun, a master wood-carver. He's carving a male Epa mask for the Epa festival. Woodcarvers are called Onishona (people who make art). They carve masks and figures for the Yoruba gods and goddesses and for shrines and festivals.

Woodcarving is an important job. It's only done by men and it takes a long time to learn. George began when he was 10 years old and trained under a master woodcarver until he was 26. Now he has his own assistant to train.

George has made many carvings for Yoruba festivals and shrines, including Epa masks, Ogboni drums, warriors on horseback, hunters, women worshipping the Goddess Oshun, and many ceremonial objects.

When Father Kevin Carroll, a Roman Catholic priest, saw George's work, he liked it very much. He asked George to do some woodcarvings for the Catholic church.

This is a scene showing the Three Kings bringing gifts to Mary and the baby Jesus. It is part of the carved wooden doors which George made for the church at Osi-Illorin.

Now George carves for both the Catholic church and the Yoruba religion. But after George became a Christian, he no longer believed that the spirits of gods lived in the Yoruba masks and figures.

Other jobs in the village done only by men are cobbler, blacksmith, and carpenter.

Some crafts, like weaving, are only done by women. Mothers teach their daughters to weave.

Afolabi, Chief Afolayan's fifth wife, is a very good weaver. Sometimes she weaves plain cloth, and other times she weaves cloth with many different colors and patterns.

When she finishes a piece of cloth, Afolabi takes it to a tailor who lives nearby. He has a sewing machine and makes the cloth into clothes for the family. All the wives take turns weaving cloth in between their other work.

In Aye-Ekan, people make almost everything they need, from clothes to houses.

Pottery is another craft which only women do. Adeola Babaola has taught her daughter how to make pots. Now the two of them always work together.

The pots are made of clay and dried in the sun. Then they're baked in a fire at the back of the house so they will be hard and strong. Later they are covered in liquid made from locust beans. This makes them black and shiny.

Adeola Babaola and her daughter make pots of all different sizes. Big pots are used for storing water or cooking yams, and tiny pots are used for medicine.

They sell their pots in the market at Aye-Ekan. People come from miles away to buy them.

Thaddeus doesn't live in Aye-Ekan all of the time. Chief Afolayan owns two houses. Besides the main family house at Aye-Ekan, with two acres of land, there is a smaller farmhouse in the forest with four acres of land.

During the school year Thaddeus lives at Aye-Ekan, but during vacations he goes to the farmhouse to help with the farmwork. It's about 15 miles (25 kilometers) away, near another village. The children take the bus part of the way and then walk the rest of the way through the forest.

Thaddeus likes living on the farm. When he isn't working in the fields or helping in the house, he plays. He's made a slingshot, called *kanna-kanna*, and uses it to shoot squirrels, birds, and bushrats.

Chief Afolayan is getting too old for hard work, so Andrew, his oldest son, is in charge of most of the farm work. Andrew and his family live on the farm almost all of the time. So do the chief's youngest wives, Afolabi and Kolajo. They watch the children, carry water and firewood, and cook the food.

21

All the vegetables the family needs are grown on the farm. Yams, corn, and cassava are the main crops. The cassava plant is grown for its roots, which are usually ground up into flour. The yam plant is a vine, with the yams growing underground like potatoes.

Other crops include okra, peppers, and tomatoes. Banana trees, oil-palm trees, and kola-nut trees also grow on the farm.

Thaddeus and his brothers work from Monday through Saturday and have Sunday off. They help plant, weed, and harvest yams and corn.

There are two main seasons in Yorubaland. The rainy season lasts from mid-March through September. The dry season begins in October and lasts until mid-March. During the rainy season, the weeds in the yam plots grow very fast, so Thaddeus and his brothers spend a lot of time weeding. For most jobs they use a hoe or a cutlass, which is a long wide knife. The farm has no tractors or machines.

Chief Afolayan doesn't farm all six acres of his land at the same time. He grows crops on one part of the land for two years. Then he lets that part rest, or lie fallow, for a year while he uses another part of his land. He also clears new areas of forest for growing crops. After a year, he can go back to using the first plot of land again. This is called crop rotation.

At the end of the summer vacation, Thaddeus and his brothers go back to Aye-Ekan for school. They go to St. Michael's Roman Catholic Primary School.

Each morning, they walk about a half an hour to get there. All the students at the school wear uniforms. Boys wear blue shirts and tan shorts, and girls wear blue dresses.

Only Catholic children can go to St. Michael's. There's another school in the village for Muslim children, and also a school run by the government.

When Thaddeus was born, his mother and father had him christened so that he could go to St. Michael's School. He started school when he was 6 years old.

During the first few days, all of the pupils help with the work around the school. The boys cut the long grass with cutlasses and the girls weed the paths. Then the children move the desks and chairs into the right classrooms. Class begins on the following Monday.

Thaddeus likes school. He is learning English, arithmetic, health education, Yoruba, art, and social studies, including history and geography. He also has lessons on the Bible and learns about nature.

His favorite subject is arithmetic. He likes doing calculations.

Thaddeus's teacher is Mr. Alufa. He was born in Aye-Ekan but has traveled all over Nigeria. When he was training to be a teacher, Mr. Alufa lived in Lagos, the capital of Nigeria. Lagos is a big modern city on the south coast, a long way from Aye-Ekan.

Mr. Alufa came back to Ake-Ekan to teach because Lagos was too crowded and busy for him. Once most of the people in Nigeria were farmers like Thaddeus's family. But during the 1960s and 1970s, more oil was found in Nigeria. People started to work in the oil industry instead of on farms.

Because of its oil, Nigeria has become one of the richest countries in Africa. But now there aren't enough farmers to produce food for the whole country. Nigeria must buy food from other countries. Both food and clothing have become very expensive, even in Aye-Ekan. Nigeria's oil hasn't helped the farmers at all. Most of the people who earn high wages live in towns.

When Thaddeus is older, he will probably go to the University of Lagos to study. His family hopes that he will become a doctor or an engineer. They'd like him to learn to do something besides farm. But Thaddeus's mother Aransi says she doesn't really mind what he chooses to do, as long as he is happy.

Yoruba People and Their Families

Yorubaland, the area in which the Yoruba group of people live, is located mainly in southwestern Nigeria. At least half the people live in towns, but many Yoruba families live in villages like Aye-Ekan.

Yoruba men usually have more than one wife. If he is Christian, a Yoruba man may have only one wife. Most Yoruba men have two wives, but some have four, and others, like Chief Afolayan, have six.

Several families live in a single compound. They are likely to be distantly related and, therefore, members of one extended family. The traditional compound consists of a large yard, with single-story houses all around it. There are 44 members in Chief Afolayan's family compound and 13 compounds in the village of Aye-Ekan.

Within the home the man is master. His senior wife also has authority over the others. She helps the younger wives and teaches them how to bring up their children. Each wife has private living quarters for herself and her children.

Children are brought up to respect their elders. They feel close to their families and share the responsibility for members of their extended family.

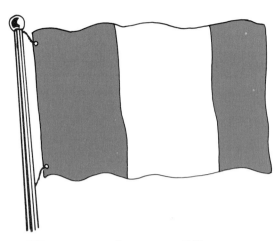

Facts about Nigeria

Capital: Lagos
A new capital is being built in the city of Abuja, in central Nigeria. When it is ready, Abuja will be the capital instead of Lagos.

Official Language: English
English is not, however, the most common language spoken. Most people speak the language of their group, such as Yoruba, Hausa, or Ibo.

Form of Money: the naira

Area: 356,669 square miles (923,768 square kilometers)
Nigeria is about one-tenth the size of the United States.

Population: about 90 million people
The population of Nigeria is about one-third that of the United States.

NORTH
AMERICA

SOUTH
AMERICA

EUROPE

A S I A

AFRICA

Nigeria

AUSTRALIA

31

Families the World Over

Some children in foreign countries live like you do. Others live very differently. In these books, you can meet children from all over the world. You'll learn about their games and schools, their families and friends, and what it's like to grow up in a faraway land.

A FAMILY IN CHINA
A FAMILY IN EGYPT
A FAMILY IN FRANCE
A FAMILY IN INDIA
A FAMILY IN JAMAICA
A FAMILY IN NIGERIA

A FAMILY IN PAKISTAN
A FAMILY IN SRI LANKA
A FAMILY IN WEST GERMANY
AN ABORIGINAL FAMILY
AN ARAB FAMILY
AN ESKIMO FAMILY

Lerner Publications Company
241 First Avenue North
Minneapolis, Minnesota 55401